Wit & Humour
DOGS

Kaye Neane

BRADWELL
BOOKS

Published by Bradwell Books
9 Orgreave Close Sheffield S13 9NP
Email: books@bradwellbooks.co.uk
Compiled by Kaye Neane

All rights reserved. No part of this publication may be reproduced, stored in a retrieval system or transmitted in any form or by any means, electronic, mechanical, photocopying, recording or otherwise without the prior permission of Bradwell Books.

British Library Cataloguing in Publication Data: a catalogue record
for this book is available
from the British Library.
1st Edition
ISBN: 9781910551271

Design by: Jenks Design
Illustrations: Tim O'Brien 2015
Print: Gomer Press, Llandysul, Ceredigion SA44 4JL

A humorous look at our relationship with Man's best friend, the humble hound, and his worst enemy, the fickle feline…

"Dogs have owners; cats have staff." Anon.

Q: Why do dogs wag their tails?
A: "Because no one else will do it for them!"

Wit & Humour/DOGS

A man went to visit a friend and was amazed to find him playing chess with his dog. He watched the game in astonishment for a while.

"I can hardly believe my eyes!" he exclaimed. "That's the cleverest dog I've ever seen."

"Nah, he's not that clever," said his friend, "I've beaten him three games out of five."

The favourite whippet racing at Stockton-on-Tees is well ahead of the field. Suddenly he's hit on the head by a free-range turkey and a dozen mince pies. He can't help himself so he bites a leg off the turkey but he manages to pull back into the lead, only to be struck by a box of Christmas crackers and a string of sausages as he rounds the bend. With great skill the dog manages to eat the sausages and get to the front of the field once more then, on the home straight, he's struck on the head by a bottle of sherry and a Christmas pudding. Thus distracted, the dog comes in second. Furious, his owner immediately goes to the stewards to complain that his whippet has been seriously hampered.

A dog turns up for a job interview and is asked, "Can you speak any foreign languages?"

"maiow," he replied.

Q: What is it called when a cat wins a dog show?
A: A CAT-HAS-TROPHY!

Q: What dog wears contact lenses?
A: A cock-eyed spaniel!

Q: What do you get if you cross a cocker spaniel, a poodle and a rooster?
A: Cockerpoodledoo!

A three-legged dog walks into a Wild West saloon bar and says to the bartender, "I'm lookin' for the guy who shot my paw."

A man with a Doberman Pinscher and a man with a Chihuahua are out for a walk and fancy something to eat. The man with the Doberman Pinscher says to his mate with the Chihuahua, "Let's go to that nice restaurant over there and get a meal."

The man with the Chihuahua says, "We can't go in there. We've got dogs with us."

The man with the Doberman Pinscher says, "It'll be OK. Just follow my lead."

They walk over to the restaurant. The man with the Doberman Pinscher puts on a pair of dark glasses, and he starts to go in.

At the door, the Maître D says, "Sorry, sir, no pets allowed." The man with the Doberman Pinscher says, "You don't understand. This is my guide dog."

The Maitre D says, "But he's a Doberman Pinscher?"

"Yes," says the man, "They're using them now, they're very good."

"Do come in then, sir," says the Maître D.

The man with the Chihuahua thinks, "Why not?" He puts on a pair of dark glasses and starts to walk in too.

"Sorry, sir, no pets allowed," says the Maitre D.

"You don't understand," says the bloke with the Chihuahua, "This is my guide dog."

"A Chihuahua?!" says the Maitre D.

"You mean the so-and-sos gave me a Chihuahua!?" exclaims the man.

With the ever increasing fashion for mixing up breeds, here are a few humorous takes on what can be done.

Collie + Lhasa Apso = Collapso, a dog that folds up for easy transport

Great Pyrenees + Dachshund = Pyradachs, a puzzling breed

Deerhound + Terrier = Derriere, a dog that's true to the end

Wit & Humour/DOGS

Pointer + Setter = Pointsetter, a traditional Christmas pet

Newfoundland + Basset Hound = Newfound Asset Hound, a dog for financial advisors

Terrier + Bulldog = Terribull, a dog that makes awful mistakes

Bull Terrier + Shitzu = Oh, never mind....

Malamute + Pointer = Moot Point, owned by.... oh, well, it doesn't matter anyway

Pekingese + Lhasa Apso = Peekasso, an abstract dog

Collie + Malamute = Commute, a dog that travels to work

Retriever + Irish Setter = Resetter, a dog that can reboot your computer

Bloodhound + Labrador = Blubador, a dog that cries at the slightest thing

Q: What do you call a large dog that meditates?
A: Aware wolf.

Q: How did the little Scottish dog feel when he saw a monster?
A: Terrier-fied!

Q: What do you call a black Eskimo dog?
A: A dusky husky.

In the staff canteen, Jack was always showing Bob photos of his dog and saying how clever it was: doing tricks, playing ball, bringing his newspaper and slippers. One day Jack brought in the album from his daughter's wedding so Bob could look through the photos.

Bob decided to tease Jack a little and said, "Hang on, where's your precious dog? I'm surprised he wasn't the Best Man!"

Jack looked at Bob as if he was stupid, "Don't be daft, someone had to take the photos."

"Dogs come when they're called. Cats take a message and get back to you later." Mary Bly

Q: What do you call a frozen dog?
A: A pupsicle.

"Some people say that cats are sneaky, evil, and cruel. True, and they have many other fine qualities as well." Missy Dizick

Q: What's happening when you hear "Woof... splat... meow... splat?"
A: It's raining cats and dogs.

Q: What do you get if you cross a Rottweiller and a hyena?
A: I don't know but I'll join in if it laughs.

Two men were walking through a really tough council estate when an enormous Pitbull Terrier emerged from behind some rubbish bins no more than 30 feet in front of them. The first man dropped his backpack and dug out a pair of running shoes, then, with trembling fingers, he began furiously to lace them up as the Pitbull slowly approached, its huge teeth bared, saliva dripping from its jaws.

The second man looked at him in confusion and said, "What are you doing? Running shoes aren't going to help. You can't outrun that dog."

"I don't need to," said the first man, "I just need to outrun you."

Q: What did the dog do in Egypt?
A: Barkeology

"My goal in life is to be as good a person as my dog already thinks I am." Anon

Man: "I have a dog that doesn't have a nose."
His mate: "And how does he smell?"
Man: "Awful."

Q: What happened when the dog went to the flea circus?
A: He stole the show!

Q: What is the dog's favorite city?
A: New Yorkie!

Q: Who is the dog's favorite comedian?
A: Growlcho Marx!

Q: Why did the dog cross the road?
A: To get to a "barking" space!

Q: What kind of dog does Dracula have?
A: A Bloodhound.

Q: What's the difference between a new husband and a new dog?
A: After a year, the dog is still excited to see you.

Someone left the front door open accidentally and Sam's dog, Rover, took the opportunity to go walkies. Sam realised Rover had gone and went out in the street whistling and calling his name. There was no response so Sam got in the car, drove around looking for Rover. He drove round and round for some time with no luck. Finally he pulled up alongside a couple out for a stroll and asked if they had seen his dog. They looked amused and asked, "Would that be the one running behind your car?"

A man's car stalls on a country road in Gwent. When he gets out to fix it, a Border Collie in the nearby farmyard comes up alongside and jumps up on the wall.

"Your trouble is probably with the injectors," says the dog. Startled, the man jumps back and runs down the road until he meets a farmer. He tells the farmer his story.

"Was it a black and white Collie with a black mark over the right eye?" asks the farmer.

"Yes, yes," the agitated man replies.

"Oh, I wouldn't listen to him," says the farmer, "he don't know a thing about cars."

"I got rid of my husband," said the lady at lunch, "The dog was allergic."

Q: What do you get when you cross a dog and a calculator?
A: A friend you can count on.

"Women and cats will do as they please, and men and dogs should relax and get used to the idea." Robert A. Heinlein

The woman approached the policeman, crying her eyes out, and said that her dog, Fido, was lost. When he suggested that she put an ad in the paper, the woman replied, "Well, I thought of that, officer, but then I remembered that dear little Fido can't read."

Q: What do you get if you cross a gold dog with a telephone?
A: A golden receiver!

A man walks past a pet store in Lancaster. There is a sign in the window that says TALKING DOG FOR SALE.

The man doesn't believe it, but he is curious so he goes into the store. He sees a Staffordshire Terrier, walks up to the dog and says, "Alright, kidda?"

The dog says, "Ah do, youth? How bin yer?"

The man says "By gum! Tha canst really talk!"

The dog says, "That's right, kidda"

The man says, "So what is it like being a talking dog?"

The dog says, "Well, I've lived a fine, full life. I rescued Avalanche victims in The Alps. I worked as a drug-sniffing dog for the FBI, and now I read to people in an old folks home five days a week."

The man is absolutely amazed. He turns to the owner of the pet shop and says, "Hecky-pecky! Why would you sell a dog like this???"

The pet shop owner says, "Because he's a great big liar! He never did ANY of those things."

Q: What did the skeleton say to the puppy?
A: Bon appetite

Q: What do you get if you cross a Beatle and an Australian dog?
A: Dingo Starr

Q: What do you get if you cross a sheepdog with a jelly?
A: The collie wobbles!

A farmer is wondering how many sheep he has in his field, so he asks his sheepdog to count them. The dog runs into the field, counts them, and then runs back to his master.

"So," says the farmer. "How many sheep were there?"

"40," replies the dog.

"How can there be 40?" exclaims the farmer. "I only bought 38!"

"I know," says the dog. "But I rounded them up."

Q: What do you call a dog magician?
A: A labracadabrador.

Q: What did the cowboy say when the bear ate Lassie?
A: "Well, doggone!"

A burglar broke into a house one night. He shone his torch around, looking for valuables, and when he picked up a CD player to place in his sack, a strange, disembodied voice echoed from the dark saying, "Mother is watching you".

He nearly jumped out of his skin, clicked his torch off and froze. When he heard nothing more after a bit, he shook his head, promised himself a vacation after the next big score, then clicked the light back on and began searching more valuables. Just as he pulled the stereo out so he could disconnect the wires, clear as a bell he heard, "Mother is watching you." Totally rattled, he shone his light around frantically, looking for the source of the voice.

Finally, in the corner of the room, his torch beam came to rest on a parrot.

"Did you say that?" he hissed at the parrot.

"Yes," the parrot squawked, "I'm just trying to warn you."

The burglar relaxed. "Warn me, huh? Who do you think you are any way?"

"Daddy," replied the bird.

"Daddy," the burglar laughed. "What kind of stupid people would name a parrot 'Daddy'?"

The bird promptly answered, "The same kind of people who would name a Rottweiler 'Mother'!"

Wit & Humour/DOGS

Q: How can tell if you have a stupid dog?
A: It chases parked cars!

Labrador: "How's your human?"
Doberman: "Still following me around with a plastic bag picking up my doings."
Labrador: "Yeah, mine too. Still it seems to make them happy."

A woman saw an ad in the local newspaper which read: "Purebred Police Dog £25."

Thinking that was a great bargain, she called and ordered the dog to be delivered.

The next day a van arrived at her home and delivered the mangiest-looking mongrel she had ever seen.

In a rage, she telephoned the man who had placed the ad, "How dare you call that mangy-mutt a purebred police dog?"
"Don't let his looks deceive you, ma'am," the man replied, "He's undercover."

Q: What is a dog's favorite sport?
A: Long distance drooling!

Q: What do you get if you take a really big dog out for a walk?
A: A Great Dane out!

"Cats are smarter than dogs. You can't get eight cats to pull a sled through snow." Jeff Valdez

In front of the local pet shop, an antique collector noticed a mangy little puppy eating dog food from a saucer. The saucer, he realised with a start, was a rare and precious piece of Meissen porcelain – a valuable collector's item.

The man strolled into the shop and offered two pounds for the puppy.

"He's not for sale", said the shopkeeper.

"Look", said the collector, "that puppy is dirty and scabby, but I feel sorry for him.

I'll raise my offer to ten pounds".

"It's a deal", said the proprietor, and pocketed the tenner immediately.

"For that amount of money I'm sure you won't mind throwing in the saucer," said the connoisseur, "The puppy seems so happy drinking from it.'

"I can't do that," said the shopkeeper firmly, "That's my lucky saucer.

From that saucer, I've sold 18 dogs already this week."

Q: When does a dog go "miaow"?
A: When it is learning a new language.

Q: Why did the poor dog chase his own tail?
A: He was trying to make both ends meet.

Q: Where does a Rottweiller sit in the cinema?
A: Anywhere it wants…

Q: How are a dog and a marine biologist alike?
A: One wags a tail and the other tags a whale.

Q: What is a dog's favorite food?
A: Anything that's on your plate!

"If animals could speak, the dog would be a blundering outspoken fellow; but the cat would have the rare grace of never saying a word too much." Mark Twain

A local business was looking for office help. They put a sign in the window, stating the following: "HELP WANTED. Must be able to type, be good with data sets and must be bilingual. We are an Equal Opportunities Employer."

A short time afterwards, a dog trotted up to the window, saw the sign and went inside. He looked at the receptionist and wagged his tail, then walked over to the sign, looked at it and whined. Getting the idea, the receptionist got the office manager.

The office manager looked at the dog in surprise. However, the dog looked determined, so he led him into the office. Inside, the dog jumped up on the chair and stared at the manager.

The manager said, "I can't hire you. The sign says you have to be able to type."

The dog jumped down, went to the computer and proceeded to type out a perfect letter. He took out the page, trotted over to the manager, gave it to him, and jumped back on the chair.
The manager was stunned, but told the dog, "The sign says you have to be good with data sets."

The dog jumped down again and went to the computer. The dog proceeded to input a complex series of data sets that produced perfect pivot tables. He wagged his tail and looked at the manager expectantly.

By this time the manager was totally dumb-founded. He looked at the dog and said, "I realise that you are a very intelligent dog and have some interesting abilities. However, I still can't give you the job."

The dog jumped down, left the office then came back with the sign in his mouth. He put his paw on the sentence about Equal Opportunities.

The manager said, "Yes, but the sign also says that you have to be bilingual."

The dog looked at the manager calmly and said, "Miaow."

Q: What do you get if you cross a dog and a cheetah?
A: A dog that chases cars – and catches them!

Q: What is the favourite dog in North Korea?
A: A sausage dog.

"The cat could very well be man's best friend but would never stoop to admitting it." Doug Larson

Wit & Humour/DOGS

Two Alsatian bitches are sitting on the front porch passing the time of day when a really handsome Alsatian walks by and winks at them.

"Oh darling, did you see that one?" one of the bitches.

"I wouldn't mind sharing a can of Ken-o-meat with him."

"Oh, forget about him, sweetie," says her friend. "I went out with him once, and all he did was talk about his operation."

Q: What do you get if you cross a dog and a lion?
A: A terrified postman.

Police officer: "Excuse me, but your dog has been chasing a man on his bicycle."
Dog owner: "Are you crazy? My dog can't even ride a bicycle."

Wit & Humour/DOGS

A man in the cinema notices what looks like a spaniel sitting next to him.

"Are you a dog?" asks the man, surprised.

"Yes," says the spaniel.

"What are you doing watching a movie?" asks the man.

"Well, I liked the book," the spaniel replies.

Q: What do you call a dog with a surround sound system?
A: A sub-woofer.

Q: What's more amazing than a talking dog?
A: A Spelling Bee.

Q: What did the hungry Dalmatian say when he had a meal?
A: That hit the spot!

Q: What happened to the dog that ate nothing but garlic?
A: His bark was much worse than his bite!

Wit & Humour/DOGS

Q: Where do dogs go after their tails fall off?
A: The re-tail store.

"If a dog jumps into your lap it is because he is fond of you; but if a cat does the same thing it is because your lap is warmer." A. N. Whitehead

Q: What's a dog favorite hobby?
A: Collecting fleas!

An avid duck hunter was in the market for a new bird dog. His search ended when he found a dog that could actually walk on water to retrieve a duck. Shocked by his find, he was sure none of his friends would ever believe him.

He decided to break the news to a friend of his, a pessimist by nature, and invited him to hunt with him and his new dog.

As they waited by the shore, a flock of ducks flew by. They fired, and a duck fell. The dog responded and jumped onto the water. The dog did not sink but instead glided across the water to retrieve the bird, never getting more than his paws wet. The friend saw everything but did not say a single word.

On the drive home the hunter asked his friend, "Did you notice anything unusual about my new dog?" "Yeah," said his mate. "He can't swim."

"In ancient times cats were worshipped as gods; they have not forgotten this." Terry Pratchett

A blind man is at the optician's with his guide dog. Both are facing the eye test chart on the wall. The optician takes the guide dog away, replaces it with another guide dog, and asks, "Is that better or worse?"

How many Dogs does it take to Change a Light Bulb?

Alsatian: Alright, everyone stop where you are! Who broke the light bulb? I SAID, "STOP WHERE YOU ARE!"

Australian Shepherd: First, I'll put all the light bulbs in a circle…

Boxer: Who cares? I can still play with my squeaky toys in the dark.

Cocker Spaniel: Why change it? I can still pee on the carpet in the dark.

Dachshund: It's your light bulb, you change it.

Golden Retriever: The sun is shining, the day is young, we've got our whole lives ahead of us, and you're inside worrying about a light bulb?

Greyhound: It isn't moving. Who cares?

Hound Dog: ZZZZZZZZZzzzzzzzzz

Jack Russell: I'll just pop it in while I'm bouncing off the walls and furniture.

Lab: Oh, me, me! Pleeeeeeze let me change the light bulb! Can I? Can I? Huh? Huh? Huh? Can I?

Malamute: Let the Border Collie do it. You can feed me while he's busy.

Pointer: I see it, there it is, there it is, right there.

Poodle: Not me, I'm drying my nails.

Rottweiler: Make me.

A butcher is busy at work when notices a dog in his shop. He shoos the dog away. Ten minutes later, the dog is back again. The butcher notices that the dog has a note in his mouth. He takes the note which reads: Can I have 12 sausages and a leg of lamb, please.

The butcher looks and sees a £10 note in the dog's mouth. He takes the money, puts the sausages and lamb in a bag, and places it in the dog's mouth.

The butcher is very impressed and, since it's closing time, he decides to shut the shop and follow the dog. Down the street, the dog comes to a crossing, puts down the bag, jumps up and presses the crossing button. Then he waits patiently, bag in mouth, for the lights to change then walks across the road, with the butcher following. The dog comes to a bus stop and starts looking at the timetable. The dog checks out the times and sits on a seat to wait for the bus. The butcher is in awe.

Along comes a bus. The dog looks at the number and goes back to his seat. Another bus comes. Again the dog looks at the number; this time he climbs on. The butcher follows him, open-mouthed. The bus travels out to the suburbs. Eventually the dog gets up, stands on his hind legs and pushes the bell. The dog gets off the bus, the butcher still following.

The dog approaches a house, walks up the path, and drops the shopping on the step. Then he walks back down the

path, takes a big run, and throws himself WHAP! against the door. He takes another run, and throws himself WHAP! against the door again! There's no answer, so the dog jumps up on a narrow wall and walks to a window. He bangs his head against it several times, then jumps off the wall, and waits at the door.

A big bloke opens the door and starts shouting at the dog really loudly. He lifts his foot to kick him but the butcher runs up and stops him.

"What the heck are you doing? This dog is a genius. He could be on TV, he's so clever!"

"Clever? My arm!" the man shouts, "This is the second time this week he's forgotten his key!"